# UTE

Big Buddy Books
An Imprint of Abdo Publishing
abdopublishing.com

Katie Lajiness

**abdopublishing.com**

Published by Abdo Publishing, a division of ABDO, PO Box 398166, Minneapolis, Minnesota 55439.
Copyright © 2019 by Abdo Consulting Group, Inc. International copyrights reserved in all countries. No part
of this book may be reproduced in any form without written permission from the publisher. Big Buddy Books™
is a trademark and logo of Abdo Publishing.

Printed in the United States of America, North Mankato, Minnesota.
052018
092018

Cover Photo: David W. Hamilton/Alamy Stock Photo.
Background Photo: Efrain Padro/Alamy Stock Photo.
Interior Photos: bauhaus1000/Getty Images (p. 11); Corey Ford/Getty Images (p. 23); David W. Hamilton/Getty
    Images (p. 5); Ida C. Shum/Getty Images (p. 25); John Parrot/Getty Images (p. 27); JT Vintage/Alamy Stock
    Photo (p. 13); Ken Canning/Getty Images (p. 21); Marilyn Angel Wynn/Native Stock (pp. 9, 15, 16, 17, 19,
    26, 29, 30).

Coordinating Series Editor: Tamara L. Britton
Contributing Editor: Jill Roesler
Graphic Design: Jenny Christensen, Maria Hosley

Library of Congress Control Number: 2017962684

Publisher's Cataloging-in-Publication Data

Name: Lajiness, Katie, author.
Title: Ute / by Katie Lajiness.
Description: Minneapolis, Minnesota : Abdo Publishing, 2019. | Series: Native Americans
    set 4 | Includes online resources and index.
Identifiers: ISBN 9781532115127 (lib.bdg.) | ISBN 9781532155840 (ebook)
Subjects: LCSH: Ute Indians--Juvenile literature. | Indians of North America--Juvenile
    literature. | Indigenous peoples--Social life and customs--Juvenile literature. |
    Cultural anthropology--Juvenile literature.
Classification: DDC 970.00497--dc23

# CONTENTS

# AMAZING PEOPLE

Hundreds of years ago, North America was mostly wild, open land. Native American tribes lived on the land. Each has its own language and **customs**.

The Ute (YOOT) are one Native American tribe. Many know them for their **ceremonies** and handmade crafts. Let's learn more about these Native Americans.

## Did You Know?

The name *Ute* means "high land" or "land of the sun."

Today, the Ute continue to gather at Ute Mountain Tribal Park in Colorado.

# Ute Territory

Ute homelands were in what is now Colorado and Utah. Over time, the tribe spread to New Mexico, Arizona, and Wyoming. While the Ute lived in different areas, they all spoke the same language.

Long ago, the Ute tribe was made up of seven to 12 different groups called bands. Today, there are three main bands. They are the Northern Ute, the Southern Ute, and the Mountain Ute.

CANADA

UNITED STATES

## UTE HOMELANDS

WYOMING

NEBRASKA

UTAH

COLORADO

KANSAS

ARIZONA

NEW MEXICO

OKLAHOMA

MEXICO

N
W    E
S

# Home Life

The Ute built different kinds of homes. Their homes were easy to take down, move, and rebuild.

Many lived in domed houses called wickiups. These homes were about eight feet (2 m) high and 15 feet (5 m) around.

Tribe members also used sweathouses. They poured water over heated rocks to make steam. This warm air caused people to sweat, which cleaned their skin.

Some Utes built cone-shaped homes made with branches, bark, reeds, and grasses. In wintertime, they covered these homes with elk or buffalo hides.

# What They Ate

Food was limited for the Ute. They traveled across large areas to find it.

During the 1600s, the Ute began riding horses. This way, they were better able to hunt antelope, buffalo, and elk.

Women gathered berries, nuts, roots, and seeds. They also mixed dried crickets and grasshoppers with berries to make cakes.

Ute men hunted year round. They wore snowshoes to hunt through deep snow.

# Daily Life

The Ute wore clothes made from the hides of deer, mountain sheep, and antelope.

Men wore long shirts, leggings, and moccasins. Some men pierced their noses and filled the hole with an animal bone. And many painted their bodies and faces.

Women wore long dresses made of deer hides. Sometimes, they added feathered headbands. Ute women wore leggings sewn to moccasins. They parted their hair in the middle. Sometimes, they wore necklaces made of seeds and stones.

Men kept their hair in two braids. They sometimes tied fur into their braids.

Parents, children, and grandparents lived in one home. Together, the adults cared for the children. Women were in charge of the home and cooking the food. They also made baskets and clothes.

Men hunted animals and protected the village from enemies. Children helped adults gather food.

Girls helped their mothers care for babies by carrying the young on cradleboards.

# Made by Hand

The Ute made many objects by hand. They often used natural supplies. These arts and crafts added beauty to everyday life.

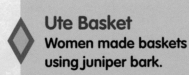

**Ute Basket**
Women made baskets using juniper bark.

### Beaded Horse on Bag
The Southern Ute used beads to design bags.

 ### Stone Figures
The tribe members formed religious charms using stone or clay.

 ### Petroglyph of Ute Man Hunting
The Ute created some of the world's first artwork by carving characters into rocks.

# Spirit Life

In a famous Ute story, a bear taught a tribal hunter to **perform** a **religious** dance. The bear told the man to teach it to the Ute people. Today, the Ute still perform the Bear Dance. They believe it helps them gain strength and let go of their worries.

The oldest Ute ceremony is the Bear Dance. Every spring, they perform short dances to honor the grizzly bear.

# STORYTELLERS

Stories were important to the Ute. In their creation story, a coyote challenged the Creator by opening a magic bag. The Ute people escaped from the bag. They ran away and spread throughout the land.

Coyotes once made the Creator mad. So, the Creator cursed them to walk on four legs.

# Fighting for Land

   Throughout history, the Ute fought for their rights. During the 1540s, Spanish **explorers** entered the American Southwest. The Spanish took control of the Ute.

   The Ute learned about horses while held as Spanish **captives**. When the Ute escaped, they took horses with them into the High Plains. The use of horses meant the Ute could travel farther away from their villages.

   In 1865, the Western Ute met **Mormons** coming to Utah. The tribe was overcome by more than 300 Mormon communities in the United States, Mexico, and Canada.

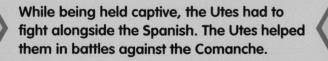

While being held captive, the Utes had to fight alongside the Spanish. The Utes helped them in battles against the Comanche.

23

In 1878, the US government withheld food and supplies until the Ute agreed to become farmers. The next year, the Ute attacked US soldiers.

The battle ended a week later when Ute chiefs ordered the tribe to give up. But many people died in the battle.

In 1881, the US Army forced the Ute out of Colorado. They had to go to a **reservation** in Utah.

Garden of the Gods is in Colorado. The area used to be a Ute religious site. Today, it is a national landmark.

# BACK IN TIME

### 1650s

The Ute met the Spanish. They also began hunting on horseback.

### 1600s

There were about 4,000 Ute in what is now the United States.

### 1821

The Mexican government granted its people land in Ute territory.

### 1861

President Abraham Lincoln gave the Ute land by creating the Uintah **Reservation** in Utah.

## 1868

The Colorado Ute signed a **treaty** with the US government. The treaty reduced the Ute's land to only 15 million acres (6 million ha).

## 1905

President Theodore Roosevelt took more than 1 million acres (400,000 ha) of land from the Ute **reservations** in Utah.

## 1924

All Native Americans born in the United States became US citizens.

## 2017

A teacher gave $250,000 to the tribe. She wanted to pay tribe members back for land her great-grandparents took years earlier.

# THE UTE TODAY

The Ute have a long, rich history. Many remember them for their ability to ride and raise horses.

Ute roots run deep. Today, the people have held on to those special things that make them Ute. Even though times have changed, many people carry the **customs**, stories, and memories of the past into the present.

## Did You Know?

Today, about 7,500 Ute live in the Colorado and Utah region.

Every year, the Ute honor their history at the Southern Ute Tribal Fair and Powwow.

"The agreement an Indian makes to a United States treaty is like the agreement a buffalo makes with his hunters when pierced with arrows."

— Chief Ouray, Ute

# GLOSSARY

**captive**  someone who is held as a prisoner or locked up.

**ceremony**  a formal event on a special occasion.

**custom**  a practice that has been around a long time and is common to a group or a place.

**explorer**  a person who travels to new or unknown places.

**Mormon**  a religious group started by Joseph Smith in 1830 in Fayette, New York.

**perform**  to do something in front of an audience.

**religious**  of or related to religion, which is the service and worship of God or the supernatural.

**reservation**  (reh-zuhr-VAY-shuhn)  a piece of land set aside by the government for Native Americans to live on.

**treaty**  an agreement made between two or more groups.

**Online Resources**

**Booklinks**
**NONFICTION NETWORK**
FREE! ONLINE NONFICTION RESOURCES

To learn more about the Ute, visit **abdobooklinks.com**. These links are routinely monitored and updated to provide the most current information available.

# INDEX